Homemade Body Butters

25 Body Butter Recipes for Amazing Skin

Copyright © 2015, Donna Summers

All rights Reserved. No part of this publication or the information in it may be quoted from or reproduced in any form by means such as printing, scanning, photocopying or otherwise without prior written permission of the copyright holder.

Disclaimer and Terms of Use:

Effort has been made to ensure that the information in this book is accurate and complete, however, the author and the publisher do not warrant the accuracy of the information, text and graphics contained within the book due to the rapidly changing nature of science, research, known and unknown facts and internet. The Author and the publisher do not hold any responsibility for errors, omissions or contrary interpretation of the subject matter herein. This book is presented solely for motivational and informational purposes only.

Table of Contents

Introduction 5

Homemade Body Butter Recipes 7

    Basic Coconut Oil Body Butter 9

    Creamy Cocoa Body Butter 11

    Easy Shea Body Butter 13

    Simple Mango Body Butter 15

    Awesome Avocado Body Butter 17

    Sun Protection Body Butter 19

    Hydrating Mango Argan Oil Body Butter 21

    Whipped Rosemary Mint Body Butter 23

    Relaxing Lavender Body Butter 25

    Detoxifying Mango Citrus Body Butter 27

    Rehydrating Rose Body Butter 29

    Refreshing Pine Forest Body Butter 31

    Cellulite-Reducing Cinnamon Body Butter 33

    Pink Peppermint Body Butter 35

    Healing Antibacterial Body Butter 37

    Fresh and Floral Body Butter 39

    Energizing Coffee Body Butter 41

    Spiced Vanilla Bean Body Butter 43

    Wrinkle-Reducing Vitamin E Body Butter 45

Holiday Spice Body Butter 47

Invigorating Lemon Cream Body Butter 49

Orange Blossom Mood-Lifting Body Butter.................. 51

Calming Chamomile Body Butter 53

Soothing Vanilla Jasmine Body Butter.......................... 55

Tropical Coconut Lime Body Butter.............................. 57

Conclusion 59

Introduction

If you want your skin to look and feel its best then you need to keep it hydrated. During the winter, cold winds can leech moisture out of your skin and, during the summer, sun damage can leave your skin feeling dry. Rather than spending a small fortune on expensive lotions and body butters at a boutique beauty shop or specialty store, why not try your hand at making your own body butters? Homemade body butters are easier to make than you might think and you don't even need any special equipment. If you are curious to try homemade body butters for yourself, this book is the perfect place to start.

Within the pages of this book you will receive twenty-five unique recipes for homemade body butters made with all-natural ingredients like coconut oil, shea butter, and essential oils. So, if you are ready to give homemade body butters a try, pick a recipe and get going!

Homemade Body Butter Recipes

Recipes Included in this Book:

Basic Coconut Oil Body Butter

Creamy Cocoa Body Butter

Easy Shea Body Butter

Simple Mango Body Butter

Awesome Avocado Body Butter

Sun Protection Body Butter

Hydrating Mango Argan Oil Body Butter

Whipped Rosemary Mint Body Butter

Relaxing Lavender Body Butter

Detoxifying Mango Citrus Body Butter

- Rehydrating Rose Body Butter
- Refreshing Pine Forest Body Butter
- Cellulite-Reducing Cinnamon Body Butter
- Pink Peppermint Body Butter
- Healing Antibacterial Body Butter
- Fresh and Floral Body Butter
- Energizing Coffee Body Butter
- Spiced Vanilla Bean Body Butter
- Wrinkle-Reducing Vitamin E Body Butter
- Holiday Spice Body Butter
- Invigorating Lemon Cream Body Butter
- Orange Blossom Mood-Lifting Body Butter
- Calming Chamomile Body Butter
- Soothing Vanilla Jasmine Body Butter
- Tropical Coconut Lime Body Butter

Basic Coconut Oil Body Butter

Ingredients:

- 1 cup organic coconut oil
- 1 teaspoon vitamin E oil

Instructions:

1. Melt the coconut oil in a double boiler over low heat.
2. Once the coconut oil is melted, remove from heat and whisk in the vitamin E oil until smooth.
3. Transfer the mixture to the refrigerator for 5 minutes to cool.
4. Remove the mixture from the refrigerator and beat with a hand mixer for 12 to 15 minutes until thick and whipped.

5. Spoon the body butter into small glass jars and store in a cool, dry location.

Creamy Cocoa Body Butter

Ingredients:

- 1 cup organic cocoa butter
- ½ cup organic coconut oil
- ½ cup sweet almond oil

Instructions:

1. Melt the cocoa butter and coconut oil in a double boiler over low heat.
2. Once the ingredients are melted, remove from heat and whisk in the sweet almond oil until smooth.
3. Transfer the mixture to the refrigerator for about 30 minutes to cool.

4. Remove the mixture from the refrigerator and beat with a hand mixer for 12 to 15 minutes until thick and whipped.
5. Spoon the body butter into small glass jars and store in a cool, dry location.

Easy Shea Body Butter

Ingredients:

- 1 cup organic shea butter
- ½ cup organic coconut oil
- ½ cup sweet almond oil

Instructions:

1. Melt the shea butter and coconut oil in a double boiler over low heat.
2. Once the butters are melted, remove from heat and whisk in the sweet almond oil.
3. Transfer the mixture to the refrigerator for 15 minutes to cool.
4. Remove the mixture from the refrigerator and beat with a hand mixer for 12 to 15 minutes until thick and whipped.

5. Spoon the body butter into small glass jars and store in a cool, dry location.

Simple Mango Body Butter

Ingredients:

- 1 cup organic shea butter
- ½ cup organic mango butter
- ½ cup sweet almond oil
- 20 drops mango essential oil

Instructions:

Melt the shea butter and mango butter in a double boiler over low heat.

Once the butters are melted, remove from heat and whisk in the sweet almond oil and mango essential oil until smooth.

Transfer the mixture to the refrigerator for 15 minutes to cool.

Remove the mixture from the refrigerator and beat with a hand mixer for 4 to 6 minutes until creamy or beat for 12 to 15 minutes until thick and whipped.

Spoon the body butter into small glass jars and store in a cool, dry location.

Awesome Avocado Body Butter

Ingredients:

- ½ cup organic shea butter
- ¼ cup organic avocado oil
- 1 teaspoon vitamin E oil
- 4 to 6 drops avocado essential oil

Instructions:

1. Melt the shea butter in a double boiler over low heat.
2. Once the shea butter is melted, remove from heat and whisk in the avocado oil, vitamin E oil, and essential oil until smooth.
3. Transfer the shea butter mixture to the refrigerator for 5 minutes to cool.

4. Remove the mixture from the refrigerator and beat with a hand mixer for 12 to 15 minutes until thick and whipped.
5. Spoon the body butter into small glass jars and store in a cool, dry location.

Sun Protection Body Butter

Ingredients:

- ½ cup magnesium oil
- ¼ cup organic coconut oil
- 3 tablespoons organic shea butter
- 2 tablespoons beeswax granules
- 1 teaspoon carrot seed oil

Instructions:

1. Melt the coconut oil, shea butter and beeswax in a double boiler over low heat.
2. Once the ingredients are melted, remove from heat and whisk in the carrot seed oil until smooth.
3. Transfer the mixture to a mixing bowl and start to beat with a hand mixer on medium speed.

4. With the mixer running, drizzle in the magnesium oil very slowly and beat until well combined.
5. Transfer the bowl to the refrigerator and chill for 15 minutes.
6. Beat the mixture again with the hand mixer until smooth and creamy.
7. Spoon the body butter into small glass jars and store in a cool, dry location.

Hydrating Mango Argan Oil Body Butter

Ingredients:

- ¾ cup organic mango butter
- ½ cup organic coconut oil
- ¼ cup organic shea butter
- ½ cup jojoba oil
- 1 teaspoon Moroccan argan oil

Instructions:

1. Melt the mango butter, coconut oil and shea butter in a double boiler over low heat.
2. Once the ingredients are melted, remove from heat and whisk in the jojoba oil and argan oil until smooth.
3. Transfer the mixture to the refrigerator for about 30 minutes to cool.

4. Remove the mixture from the refrigerator and beat with a hand mixer for 12 to 15 minutes until thick and whipped.
5. Spoon the body butter into small glass jars and store in a cool, dry location.

Whipped Rosemary Mint Body Butter

Ingredients:

- ½ cup organic shea butter
- ½ cup organic mango butter
- ½ cup organic coconut oil
- ½ cup sweet almond oil
- 15 drops rosemary essential oil
- 5 drops peppermint essential oil

Instructions:

1. Melt the shea butter, mango butter and coconut oil in a double boiler over low heat.
2. Once the ingredients are melted, remove from heat and whisk in the sweet almond oil and essential oils until smooth.

3. Transfer the mixture to the refrigerator for about 30 minutes to cool.
4. Remove the mixture from the refrigerator and beat with a hand mixer for 12 to 15 minutes until thick and whipped.
5. Spoon the body butter into small glass jars and store in a cool, dry location.

Relaxing Lavender Body Butter

Ingredients:

- ½ cup organic coconut oil
- 6 tablespoons organic cocoa butter
- 2 tablespoons sweet almond oil
- 15 drops lavender essential oil

Instructions:

1. Melt the coconut oil and cocoa butter in a double boiler over low heat.
2. Once the ingredients are melted, remove from heat and whisk in the sweet almond oil and essential oil until smooth.
3. Transfer the mixture to the refrigerator for about 30 minutes to cool.

4. Remove the mixture from the refrigerator and beat with a hand mixer for 12 to 15 minutes until thick and whipped.
5. Spoon the body butter into small glass jars and store in a cool, dry location.

Detoxifying Mango Citrus Body Butter

Ingredients:

- 1 cup organic shea butter
- ½ cup organic mango butter
- ½ cup sweet almond oil
- 1 teaspoon vitamin E oil
- 12 drops lime essential oil
- 4 drops lemon essential oil
- 4 drops bergamot essential oil

Instructions:

1. Melt the shea butter and mango butter in a double boiler over low heat.
2. Once the butters are melted, remove from heat and whisk in the sweet almond oil and essential oils until smooth.

3. Transfer the mixture to the refrigerator for 15 minutes to cool.
4. Remove the mixture from the refrigerator and beat with a hand mixer for 4 to 6 minutes until creamy or beat for 12 to 15 minutes until thick and whipped.
5. Spoon the body butter into small glass jars and store in a cool, dry location.

Rehydrating Rose Body Butter

Ingredients:

- ½ cup organic coconut oil
- 6 tablespoons organic cocoa butter
- 2 tablespoons jojoba oil
- 1 teaspoon vitamin E oil
- 15 drops rose essential oil

Instructions:

1. Melt the coconut oil and cocoa butter in a double boiler over low heat.
2. Once the ingredients are melted, remove from heat and whisk in the jojoba oil, vitamin E oil and essential oil until smooth.
3. Transfer the mixture to the refrigerator for about 30 minutes to cool.

4. Remove the mixture from the refrigerator and beat with a hand mixer for 12 to 15 minutes until thick and whipped.
5. Spoon the body butter into small glass jars and store in a cool, dry location.

Refreshing Pine Forest Body Butter

Ingredients:

- ½ cup organic shea butter
- ½ cup organic mango butter
- ½ cup organic coconut oil
- ½ cup jojoba oil
- 15 drops pine essential oil

Instructions:

1. Melt the shea butter, mango butter and coconut oil in a double boiler over low heat.
2. Once the ingredients are melted, remove from heat and whisk in the jojoba oil and pine essential oil until smooth.
3. Transfer the mixture to the refrigerator for about 30 minutes to cool.

4. Remove the mixture from the refrigerator and beat with a hand mixer for 12 to 15 minutes until thick and whipped.
5. Spoon the body butter into small glass jars and store in a cool, dry location.

Cellulite-Reducing Cinnamon Body Butter

Ingredients:

- ½ cup organic coconut oil
- ¼ cup organic shea butter
- ¼ cup organic cocoa butter
- ¼ cup witch hazel
- 2 teaspoons vitamin E oil
- 1 teaspoon ground cinnamon
- 15 drops cinnamon essential oil

Instructions:

1. Melt the shea butter, cocoa butter and coconut oil in a double boiler over low heat.
2. Once the ingredients are melted, remove from heat and whisk in the witch hazel, vitamin E oil and cinnamon essential oil until smooth.

3. Transfer the mixture to the refrigerator for about 30 minutes to cool.
4. Remove the mixture from the refrigerator and beat with a hand mixer for 12 to 15 minutes until thick and whipped.
5. Spoon the body butter into small glass jars and store in a cool, dry location.

Pink Peppermint Body Butter

Ingredients:

- ½ cup organic coconut oil
- 6 tablespoons organic cocoa butter
- 2 tablespoons sweet almond oil
- 10 drops peppermint essential oil
- 2 drops red food coloring

Instructions:

1. Melt the coconut oil and cocoa butter in a double boiler over low heat.
2. Once the ingredients are melted, remove from heat and whisk in the sweet almond oil, essential oil and food coloring until smooth.
3. Transfer the mixture to the refrigerator for about 30 minutes to cool.

4. Remove the mixture from the refrigerator and beat with a hand mixer for 12 to 15 minutes until thick and whipped.
5. Spoon the body butter into small glass jars and store in a cool, dry location.

Healing Antibacterial Body Butter

Ingredients:

- 1 cup organic shea butter
- ½ cup organic mango butter
- ½ cup jojoba oil
- 12 drops eucalyptus essential oil
- 6 drops lemongrass essential oil

Instructions:

1. Melt the shea butter and mango butter in a double boiler over low heat.
2. Once the butters are melted, remove from heat and whisk in the jojoba oil and essential oils until smooth.
3. Transfer the mixture to the refrigerator for 15 minutes to cool.

4. Remove the mixture from the refrigerator and beat with a hand mixer for 4 to 6 minutes until creamy or beat for 12 to 15 minutes until thick and whipped.
5. Spoon the body butter into small glass jars and store in a cool, dry location.

Fresh and Floral Body Butter

Ingredients:

- ½ cup organic coconut oil
- 6 tablespoons organic cocoa butter
- 2 tablespoons sweet almond oil
- 10 drops rose essential oil
- 4 drops geranium essential oil
- 2 drops jasmine essential oil

Instructions:

1. Melt the coconut oil and cocoa butter in a double boiler over low heat.
2. Once the ingredients are melted, remove from heat and whisk in the sweet almond oil and essential oils until smooth.

3. Transfer the mixture to the refrigerator for about 30 minutes to cool.
4. Remove the mixture from the refrigerator and beat with a hand mixer for 12 to 15 minutes until thick and whipped.
5. Spoon the body butter into small glass jars and store in a cool, dry location.

Energizing Coffee Body Butter

Ingredients:

- ½ cup organic coconut oil
- ½ cup beeswax granules
- 1 ½ cups hot brewed coffee

Instructions:

1. Melt the coconut oil and beeswax in a double boiler over low heat.
2. Once the ingredients are melted, remove from heat and whisk in the hot coffee.
3. Transfer the mixture to the refrigerator for about 10 minutes to cool.
4. Remove the mixture from the refrigerator and beat with a hand mixer for 12 to 15 minutes until thick and whipped.

5. Spoon the body butter into small glass jars and store in a cool, dry location.

Spiced Vanilla Bean Body Butter

Ingredients:

- 1 cup organic cocoa butter
- ½ cup organic coconut oil
- ½ cup sweet almond oil
- 1 fresh vanilla bean
- 4 drops cinnamon essential oil
- 2 drops clove essential oil

Instructions:

1. Melt the cocoa butter and coconut oil in a double boiler over low heat.
2. Once the ingredients are melted, remove from heat and whisk in the sweet almond oil and essential oils until smooth.

3. Use a sharp knife to split the vanilla bean down the middle then scrape the seeds into the blended ingredients and stir smooth.
4. Transfer the mixture to the refrigerator for about 30 minutes to cool.
5. Remove the mixture from the refrigerator and beat with a hand mixer for 12 to 15 minutes until thick and whipped.
6. Spoon the body butter into small glass jars and store in a cool, dry location.

Wrinkle-Reducing Vitamin E Body Butter

Ingredients:

- 1 cup organic shea butter
- ½ cup organic coconut oil
- ½ cup sweet almond oil
- 1 tablespoon vitamin E oil
- 10 drops geranium essential oil
- 6 drops clary sage essential oil

Instructions:

1. Melt the shea butter and coconut oil in a double boiler over low heat.
2. Once the butters are melted, remove from heat and whisk in the sweet almond oil, vitamin E oil and essential oils.

3. Transfer the mixture to the refrigerator for 15 minutes to cool.
4. Remove the mixture from the refrigerator and beat with a hand mixer for 12 to 15 minutes until thick and whipped.
5. Spoon the body butter into small glass jars and store in a cool, dry location.

Holiday Spice Body Butter

Ingredients:

- 1 cup organic cocoa butter
- ½ cup organic coconut oil
- ½ cup sweet almond oil
- 10 drops pine essential oil
- 6 drops cinnamon essential oil
- 2 drops clove essential oil
- 2 drops orange essential oil

Instructions:

1. Melt the cocoa butter and coconut oil in a double boiler over low heat.
2. Once the ingredients are melted, remove from heat and whisk in the sweet almond oil and essential oils until smooth.

3. Transfer the mixture to the refrigerator for about 30 minutes to cool.
4. Remove the mixture from the refrigerator and beat with a hand mixer for 12 to 15 minutes until thick and whipped.
5. Spoon the body butter into small glass jars and store in a cool, dry location.

Invigorating Lemon Cream Body Butter

Ingredients:

- ¾ cups organic coconut oil
- ½ cup organic cocoa butter
- 1 tablespoon vitamin E oil
- 1 teaspoon fresh lemon zest
- ½ teaspoon lemon essential oil

Instructions:

1. Melt the coconut oil and cocoa butter in a double boiler over low heat.
2. Once the ingredients are melted, remove from heat and whisk in the vitamin E oil, lemon zest, and essential oil until smooth.

3. Transfer the mixture to the refrigerator for 5 minutes to cool.
4. Remove the mixture from the refrigerator and beat with a hand mixer for 12 to 15 minutes until thick and whipped.
5. Spoon the body butter into small glass jars and store in a cool, dry location.

Orange Blossom Mood-Lifting Body Butter

Ingredients:

- ¾ cup organic shea butter
- ½ cup organic coconut oil
- ¼ cup organic mango butter
- ½ cup sweet almond oil
- 12 to 15 drops neroli essential oil
- 4 drops orange essential oil

Instructions:

1. Melt the shea butter, coconut oil and mango butter in a double boiler over low heat.
2. Once the butters are melted, remove from heat and whisk in the sweet almond oil and essential oils.

3. Transfer the mixture to the refrigerator for 15 minutes to cool.
4. Remove the mixture from the refrigerator and beat with a hand mixer for 12 to 15 minutes until thick and whipped.
5. Spoon the body butter into small glass jars and store in a cool, dry location.

Calming Chamomile Body Butter

Ingredients:

- 1 cup organic cocoa butter
- ½ cup organic coconut oil
- ½ cup jojoba oil
- 12 to 15 drops chamomile essential oil

Instructions:

1. Melt the cocoa butter and coconut oil in a double boiler over low heat.
2. Once the ingredients are melted, remove from heat and whisk in the jojoba oil and essential oil until smooth.
3. Transfer the mixture to the refrigerator for about 30 minutes to cool.

4. Remove the mixture from the refrigerator and beat with a hand mixer for 12 to 15 minutes until thick and whipped.
5. Spoon the body butter into small glass jars and store in a cool, dry location.

Soothing Vanilla Jasmine Body Butter

Ingredients:

- ½ cup organic shea butter
- ¼ cup organic avocado oil
- 1 teaspoon vitamin E oil
- ½ teaspoon vanilla extract
- 5 drops jasmine essential oil
- 2 drops vanilla essential oil

Instructions:

1. Melt the shea butter in a double boiler over low heat.
2. Once the shea butter is melted, remove from heat and whisk in the avocado oil, vitamin E oil, vanilla extract and essential oils until smooth.

3. Transfer the shea butter mixture to the refrigerator for 5 minutes to cool.
4. Remove the mixture from the refrigerator and beat with a hand mixer for 12 to 15 minutes until thick and whipped.
5. Spoon the body butter into small glass jars and store in a cool, dry location.

Tropical Coconut Lime Body Butter

Ingredients:

- 1 cup organic coconut oil
- 1 teaspoon vitamin E oil
- 1 tablespoon fresh lime zest
- 8 to 10 drops lime essential oil

Instructions:

1. Melt the coconut oil in a double boiler over low heat.
2. Once the coconut oil is melted, remove from heat and whisk in the vitamin E oil, lime zest and essential oil until smooth.
3. Transfer the mixture to the refrigerator for 5 minutes to cool.

4. Remove the mixture from the refrigerator and beat with a hand mixer for 12 to 15 minutes until thick and whipped.
5. Spoon the body butter into small glass jars and store in a cool, dry location.

Conclusion

After reading this book you should have a better understanding of how homemade body butters work. As you have learned, making homemade body butters is not very complicated and you do not need any special equipment or hard-to-find ingredients. Use your homemade body butters to restore natural hydration and beauty to your skin – they also make great gifts for friends and family! So, if you are ready to try homemade body butters for yourself then simply pick a recipe and give it a go!

Made in the USA
Las Vegas, NV
20 October 2022